FIRE

CIDER

RAIN

FIRE

CIDER

RAIN

Rhiannon Ng Cheng Hin

Coach House Books, Toronto

first edition

 Canada Council **Conseil des Arts**
for the Arts du Canada

Published with the generous assistance of the Canada Council for the Arts
and the Ontario Arts Council. Coach House Books also acknowledges the
support of the Government of Canada through the Canada Book Fund and
the Government of Ontario through the Ontario Book Publishing Tax Credit.

LIBRARY AND ARCHIVES CANADA CATALOGUING IN PUBLICATION

Title: Fire cider rain / Rhiannon Ng Cheng Hin.
Names: Ng Cheng Hin, Rhiannon, author.
Description: Poems.
Identifiers: Canadiana (print) 20220191824 | Canadiana (ebook)
20220192936 | ISBN 9781552454510 (softcover) | ISBN 9781770567443
(EPUB) | ISBN 9781770567450 (PDF)
Classification: LCC PS8627.G335 F57 2022 | DDC C811/.6—dc23

Fire Cider Rain is available as an ebook: ISBN 978 1 77056 744 3 (EPUB),
ISBN 978 1 77056 745 0 (PDF)

I want to be like water with a finger to its lips
saturated with episodes of a soul's shudder

– Don Domanski

TABLE OF CONTENTS

Part I: Evaporate

Part II: Condensate

Part III: Precipitate

Part IV: Collect

PART I

EVAPORATE

Don't civilize me with walls,
forests of lines, lanes and edges
or in roofed mazes that yawn
for my sudden death

                       – Chenjerai Hove

COEFFICIENTS OF FRICTION

MRU → *CDG* → *YYZ*

along a fibrous ridge of rain
the bodies converged   first in fields
of cloth and silk, then in lettered rows
tendons rippled on the rims of oil drums
hips trailed the hems of saltwater networks
fingers arrived raw from husking corn
in clay glades   blistered, tangential
they climbed above the clouds
the torrid rains, the kerosene lakes
the art of ambivalence
swelling   on a faint
terrestrial pulse

what breakable, half-remembered bodies
bent with small attritions
stratospheric relics gliding north
in radial heaps   away from purled trees
broken porchlights, the long ache
of the autumn island fire –
its beat, its bale, its white-tipped tongue
and thirsty, phrenic defence
gilled and wet, the clouds
swivelled up the ragged coast
the spinal tap so swift it could return
at any time, in any year, to erase
the waterlogged walk back to a place
where the erotic nature of maps
still comes as a surprise

where children spend their somnolent days
counting barnacles
in pools of earthen light

and I was there, eight, beneath a polyester blanket
watching seatbelt signs shudder in amber.

uncoil ancient oceans   peel
the skin from rust-licked coastlines
in its winged absence, absence
rinsed our paths with airwaves
sequestered them in jars
and as for the consequences
we resumed our flight rebirthed
as litmus tests for imperial decay
as architects in motion, as clusters of cells
hurtling through marginal time
which beckoned as we passed   shelve
your mothers in aerial seams   shift
toward the only life that can exist from here
the life of domesticated memory
toujours déracinée
déracinées

the wall of my styrofoam cup glistened with sea spray.

I wanted to drive the magnetic machine
through a wet-earth memory of itself   align
the hours in solar grids   return
them to their naked selves
dew-borne woman by dew-torn woman
I wanted to suspend our quivering
for one soluble second   disengage
from office life   evacuate
those bloodlines of children   collapse
one by one, the continents
to calcic dust

       sugarcane fields darkened on the underside of clouds.

somewhere over north Africa
a woman squirmed through her oval window
vaulted downward   dull pillar of light
as she fell, she cast aside those children
those lives, those artificial hours
those old coefficients of friction.
she swirled into woodland, all split hooves
mud-clawed heat, nationless
and I think I saw her years later at a gas station
in Hautes-Plaines, watching me, pleading
summoning the warmth of stucco sun –

                        I fell asleep beside Māmā.

I was aware then of what we called
dignity – the dignity of locked doors
of smashed seashells, of stray hairs and
entrances, and the overgrown dignity
of our vacated home, which groaned
as it entered the space between power
and temptation, re-entry
and radiance
as the plane pitched into descent,
the women all around me closed their eyes
and I was learning but I was impermanent
and I was holding Māmā's sleeve
and I was no longer asleep

a plexus of highways, wrecked creeks. a blinking red light.

and when that distal now arrives quickly
it carries with it the soft drift of a forgotten
hypothesis, the ocean shrivelled
to a blank seed, the whines of a rusa deer
thrashing in tall grass

eyes closed, still, the women
raise their calloused hands   stoke
the embers of the old island fire   prepare
to love their daughters   scale

the cadence of inchoate clouds:

a semi-permeable collective
at work.

SEAMELT I

in a motel room in Mahébourg,
Māmā kneels at an abacus
     counting the years between two cities.
     in the interstice, sky-ribbed
     raindrops recoil to their primordial wells
unload at the vertex of our pelagic growth
     which she resolves in whispers

     a corridor in the sky
     a corridor in the sky

memorize the smell of linen:
aquatic silk striated
     with sand, stale street names
memorize the humid pull of brine:
     the salt-stained bathtub where she grew up
     sifting saffron through each
     ceramic hour.

lamplight laps along her shadow
     real and receding, frothing in
     the hour's pores   percolate
     with all she is
     due to surrender.

she comes to bed.

     a corridor in the sky

she squeezes my hand.

we fall asleep like this
the way mothers and daughters do
the way women do
or inconsistent lovers:

      underwater weeds, tangled together
      bolting for the sun.

tulle. there is a woman, I can't remember her name. she is dead now but she is painting milkweed tulle in a kitchen stacked with lamps, chinaware, and perfumery. sun slopes away down the hall as if it will abandon itself, the honey-slit curtains, the overgrown strip of lawn, the xeric moult of insects just outside the window.

she moves in oblique brushstrokes, dull and grey-thin lines of tulle in pallid flight, in sequence, set to wind, and on the edge, the flower's viral envelope, blooming into the bloodlet of seasonal floods.

she is dead now, but she remains as a soft equatorial throb, clutching her brush with fingers so arthritic some are bent at ninety degrees to the bone. the young man comes by to trim her tiger lilies. *what are you painting?* he asks through the window. *a rebirth I saw once from a hospital window,* she responds.

the sound of clippers resumes, catches on the tip of a single air particle, rotating

suntails in the carpet.

TRICKLE DOWN

taxonomy of
time-lapsed skins
in sonorous build,
ocean liners

disperse: unattended
furls of light
in my own dimension,
origins on hold

I track women –
post-colonial eyelets
in calculated retraction,
sheltering from acid rain

rockside, nitric moss
unlocks the doors
to their childhood homes,
calls them inside

makes them hole again
as whole remains
it says,

forgive yourself for that
which you cannot salvage.

THE LAWS OF THERMODYNAMICS I

energy and matter can be neither created nor destroyed.

suspended in a water column –
three egrets, eyes green and backlit
with the mechanics of an ancient pond
what of these weightless wings

this lattice of soil, twist of gravel
necks draped on thoracic hymns
rescued from the small pities of
western life, tossed to a casual   .

roadside heap   shiver
on the cusp of polar spring
each cell a grafted pinhole of light
so small the ground nearly forgoes

its routine resuscitation
like matter, time moves only between forms
each moment a water droplet
in capillary action

cycling through salt marshes
oil slicks and seabeds   beaten
by yellowing sails and glacial bone
by the chronic flare of leaves, of

eyelashes, of sinusoidal traffic and
babies in brittle holds
seasoned by sunlight, dirt, muscle, sore

like mother like daughter like matter like water –

HUMAN DISSECTION LAB

as if by ritual, I enter a polemic
        of loss, wherein the axis of grief
lies stitched to the vein of every
        hemlock, every arthropod, every
woman's coarse throat. I swallow
        it down: in this room, the scientific
method self-immolates, skeletal
        bloodwork coalesces with latex.
her palm leaps into the sermon
        a bell hanging from each polished nail.
in hindsight, there will be motion –
        the orchids she might have loved, flourishing
on the dark side of academia
        charred inside out.
in hindsight, there will be intonation
        at the centre of her unnamed body –
a physiology swollen with letters
        that skew the hour. dictionaries pleated
into the sand.
        the words are improvised. carnal.

WHEN WÀIPÓ DIED

it was empty rooms
lifting words from
her body
methodically
gently

extracting each
in the order in
which she learned them:
the first was
mother.
the last
moth.

until her frontal lobe collapsed.

terra nullius: the inverted disposition of things
in ordinary flux, logging roads and peri-urban
lawn ornaments replicated on the clouds' nuclear
petals, I watch the patterns on her dress orbit my
eyes, my face, my mouth, overlap with auxilliary
species of our scape, a cosmic bodice, feminized
and sweating, she whispers *where do we go from here*
and we laugh. nearby: the night-stained plows on
silent hills, cropped to surveillance grids where
the diasporic tendons of our water are certified
only as incommensurable parts, split and waxed
and appropriated for the cosmetics of a *multi-
cultural nation* where one cannot be *too much of
one thing* unless that thing is a consumer.

sonar blink of microcontinents, note to self –
her hair, fingers tender in lightdrift, lunar flecks
of fabric-wet love, the arc of her neck, its lift, its
curve and buckle, its bend and heave, endemic, we

resume consumption
in this panoptical court.

OIL SPILL I

green overlaps on land   spiny skin
plows over root   so comes the fraying
the damaged instars, the browned reefs

yesterday, Māmā came over to ask if
I'd mailed that Ziploc bag of her hair
to help clean, she said,
      that damned wretched mess
on the other side of the world
and I should have told her, said,
      Māmā, Wàipó died last week
or
      I went to see her in hospital
or
      why didn't I know her better
or
      why can't you look at me
      anymore?

but she had already left.
she was forever leaving.
I go to the abscess of the lake
sunlight gets caught halfway to me

I trace lines over memories eroded by
three versions of her absence:

    i.   *a sandstone elk, sinking perpetually in the Indian Ocean*

    ii.   *my reflection in the rear-view*

    iii.   *a jar of fire cider vinegar, cracked open too soon*

SEAMELT II

4:09 a.m. (MUT)
orange peels burn outside
tektite flakes strewn on cement
kestrels perch in leafy chandeliers
sun stirs our bedsheets
with callow light

4:27 a.m. (MUT)
Māmā tries to find our grace
on the floor of this languid room
it tastes like dog mustard
contraceptives, and two hundred rupees
pressed to a stranger's tar-streaked palm

4:41 a.m. (MUT)
a corridor in the sky
she takes a shower, the sound
unclasped, the room a fluid shell
her hair splashing under salt
her dress pressurized to pulp

5:02 a.m. (MUT)
the curtain next door unravels
in blades of wind
a wedding vow slips from its folds
floats to the floor
bleaches in thin sun

5:23 a.m. (MUT)
Māmā tells the taxi driver to hurry
the convex windows of airport terminals
the sterile chaff of polyester
the footprint of an overgrown island
splayed in my eight-year-old palm

8:51 p.m. (EST)
one day – not now
I will bring myself to unlearn it all
and when I do
I will begin where she left me
with the sound of

water on tile.

PART II

CONDENSATE

Let your life lightly dance on the edges of
Time like dew on the tip of a leaf

– Rabindranath Tagore

THE LAWS OF THERMODYNAMICS II

*the total order of a system at a temperature of absolute zero is a
defined constant.*

trainlines dip along Spadina
buildings sway like orchids
on the ocean floor   gulping
against the fold of dusk
as if they have yet to live a life
of tenderness
           of shaking days with doors ajar
           of galloping, feverish storms
tell me again, the story of cartography –
           what cannot be named cannot be controlled
tell me again, how our bodies erupt –
           on street corners in boundless cities

in the streetcar, airline advertisements
shudder above my seat   mangrove inlets
gingko trees, guava-jewelled hills
pedal boats for rent
where the margin of grief begins

never mind the iron slums of Cassis
never mind that bruised atoll

I pass through saturated streets
cornea coiled over steel, over glass
over storefronts, briefcases, the pale stretch
of restraint between our lives

and yet I see her, still
between skyscrapers, traffic lights
and indivisible alleys

I am quite certain this time –
the woman who leapt from the plane
years ago   lapsing stream of light

standing alone in a distant field
frozen, eminent

activated

watching me

as sturgeons ride the ecotone beneath her feet
expanding in arboreal light.

there is a memory Māmā used to tell only in the winter, when she thought I was asleep. she would appear as a shadow in my doorway, guava juice gleaming under her fingernails.

There was this giant turtle, a one-hundred-year-old turtle that lived in the back of our cigarette shop in Port Louis. I mean not mine, my dad's, your wàigōng's. In the back back – le p'tit cou, là, with the dirt and clotheslines.

I would lie still, eyes closed.

So big you could ride it. Kids would hop the fence all the time to climb it, little bastards. Scratch its shell with a coin to make it move. Ca'a fonctionné, it worked every time. Some people think pain paralyzes you. Us islanders? We know better. We know that pain makes you move – even the memory of pain is enough to set you in motion.

sometimes the wind crackled on the windowpanes and she would pause for minutes at a time.

Papa would come out yelling and shaking a tin of coins and they'd scram. I bet if we went back now it'd still be alive… Ey but Pépin you know what I really remember? The lemon trees carved right into its shell. I'm pretty sure those things don't even grow in Mauritius. They were so detailed. So detailed. We never knew where they came from, they just showed up one day. Guess some vandal jumped the fence some night. Talented bastard though.

she did this for years. she exhumed versions of her life from the floors of cold rooms, turned them over, whispered to them, interred them again, like a child burying dead flowers.

I tell you, it was real art.

years later, the floorboards of my rooms creak, still, as I sleep, creak as I wake. she'd turn, her voice trailing down the hall.

But goddamn, that must've hurt like hell.

INTERRED

last week my neighbour shot a deer
at the edge of Lake Huron, and now
I think perhaps sinew and muscle strings
are bred to return to ash.

I can't tell:
      if your lungs are sponge, curdling
      your eyes lamplit, flickering
      if you cradled me before I knew my name
      do you remember where we came from?

to learn your anatomy is to recite
      a geometric elegy as white pines unbraid
themselves from trellised veins.
all the quiet in the woods
      is coiled through your hind legs, strained
      inside out, siphoned
                  through mirrors.

ghost of southern heat, half sun
half soil, no longer interred
by wind leaden with ginseng
only the dissonant hush
             of ice and rusted car parts.

          Wàipó's cause of death: myocardial infarction

my tender soul –
if your mouth is lined with maps of forest floors

if you know the epistemology of sunlight,
do you remember how we got here?
the boy with the rifle begins to cry.

he turns and runs, pulling time
      a hemorrhage that leaks
      into four moments:

the birth of each of his children,

      collecting old light.

ANTIPODE

oceanside markets foam on the hour's brim,
open on Grand-Baie, on a hot creole breeze

lemon pulp trails on Māmā's sandals,
rupee satchels rustle, burlap and metal

vendors arrange their fruit, wicker stalls sip
tidal light, the alley overhung with roses

this is an ecology. does an ecology defy soundwaves?
is it mine to miss? does it exist after the aisles

vacate, after truck doors slam, after I relearn
the self from which I was born running?

⁓

at the antipode, I have tried to love the cold,
these houses dulled on tepid skies

this slated city where children writhe
like crocus buds encased in ice

I am many terrible years away from sun,
sitting here on the edge of the life I envy

watching flame trees oscillate on the lake
as vanishing points merge on my eardrum

salvage clouds,
loosen their shells from serrated shorelines

pry each thread apart, search for coins
clinking on tile, for fabric rumpling,

dholl puri sizzling in oil.
soundwaves return as static on a stale current. as nothing.

Rain (*n*)
\ ˈmə-t͟hər \
1 water that descends from the clouds continuously, in a considerable quantity
2 in my late years, the ashes of a choking island fire return to me in the form of Māmā's voice – *I say this of diasporic peoples. If you must exist anywhere, if you want to make a goddamned life for yourself, let that be in the space between rainstorms,* trivial as rivulets on stiff clothing, blown in on a foiled wind

Fog drip (*n*)
\ ˈdȯ-tər \
1 droplets of fog clinging to needles or leaf tips coalesce until they are heavy enough to fall to the ground
2 I fear the most painful parts of Māmā have been lying dormant in my sacrum my entire life and my unborn children can taste them in their sleep

Deposition (*n*)
\ fər-ˈgiv-nəs \
1 a phase transition in which water vapour turns to ice, bypassing the liquid phase
2 moonlight creases on Selia's thighs. we are here again, there again, making love again in this dim apartment

Osmosis (*n*)

\ ˈmem-rē \

1   the net movement of molecules down a concentration gradient, resulting in a final state of equilibrium

2   a tropic crashing from the sky, folding itself into a brass urn

Advection (*n*)

\ ˈer-ˌplān \

1   the movement of water through the atmosphere

2   nothing arrests the code of departure – a tacit release from boat traffic, the faint moan of house lamps in the wind, tiny starlings draped over hills, aching to break loose

Canopy interception (*n*)

\ ˈwin-tər \

1   precipitation that is intercepted by plant foliage in the canopy and forest floor. it eventually evaporates back to the atmosphere before it can reach the soil

2   the refrigerator hums. snowplow lights strike the far wall of my room. I drift in and out of concentric dreams. the floorboards of my room are creaking again, creaking –

Moss (*n*)

\ ˈdir \

1   a class of bryophytic plants characterized by soft tufted stems

2   lately I have been searching for moss in the most decrepit of places: abandoned carparks, garbage dumpsters, sidewalk cracks. if there is life after death, if the sun has not given in, it will be here

Infiltration (*n*)

\ 'lāk \

1 the process by which water from the ground enters into the soil

2 occasionally, I cross paths with women who look like Māmā, like Wàipó – in Thursday evening laundromat crowds, in the temporary tumble of streetcars, in hurried sentences and vacant apologies that I cannot bring myself to recall

Snow melt (*n*)

\ milkwēd \

1 runoff produced by melting snow

2 *and listen,* she'd say as she turned off my light, *if you leave the door open wide enough, a mountain might introduce itself to you. it will teach you about centuries. how the rings in mahogany trees are made of all the world's leftover love*

Cloud (*n*)

\ Sēlēa \

1 a visible mass of condensed vapour particles, hung in the earth's atmosphere

2 the scent of seaweed on the fringes of an old memory, which arrives as a flash of warmth on the far side of a crowded lecture hall

Runoff (*n*)

\ 'mȯth \

1 the many ways in which water can move across the land

2 three moons, dipped in water, illuminating a flurry of moths as they bury themselves in my bedroom wall

Plate tectonics (*n*)

\ ˈrən \

1   water slips into the earth's mantle through tectonic plates before returning to the surface through hotspot volcanism

2   the way Wàipó smelled before she died: nectarine and formaldehyde. the way she sounded: like an animal sprinting, breathless, back into its own body.

DRY SEASON

Selia is painting the drainpipes. the hot wave of migration season comes and goes, fragrant on the burned arteries of the neighbour's rosebush, stagnant on these old rooftops where kerosene droplets hang in balance, roil with the tender rill of misplaced hours, CD cases, and Selia

is painting the drainpipes our latest respite? down the road, they're demolishing the Belleville community centre where we learned Sega on Saturdays, heels rocking on the precipice between this and some other life, now and a distant future that slides along the garden fence, milky eclipse of poolwater reflecting on back walls, mildew pulled taut by mayflies, and Selia is

painting the drainpipes has become ritualistic. sun drips cornsilk over the eaves, seeds re-enter their visceral sheaths, and I study the nervous system of the Mauritian turtle. wind threads the tassels of old magnolias like axons accelerating along bone, shooting, proliferating, reaching, grasping, and outside, Selia is painting

the drainpipes rust into late August, wavering on the colic rustle of an expired elsewhere

THE LAWS OF THERMODYNAMICS III

an isolated system possesses a natural tendency to deteriorate to
increasingly disordered states over time.

Māmā, can you sit with me here
at the back of this Greyhound,
guarded from the indifference

of elevators, of televisions, ECGs,
sterile hallways, and white envelopes
with their cold, irrefutable seals

slip over sandhills and snowy fields,
the quiet assault of highways
sit with me

and watch tail lights trickle
through southern Ontario   wobble
in the dark, a carnival of fish

piping along black sandbeds,
bioluminous, oblivious
to the great task of *belonging*, of *being*

belonging where, being what?
the amniotic bell ponds
of Pamplemousse gardens

overgrown airstrips choked
with guava, gold-yellow bracts,

soil carved into wavelets – kinetic,
forking into this distant *where,*

I am beset now with
that usual decompression sickness,
a dull measure of time passed

Māmā, tell me what it would mean
to recognize a person with no
body, no voice, skin, or tongue

when we rise with water,
how shall I find you again?
how shall I find myself again

outside of these bodies which harbour
an island nation so microscopic,
so disposable

if one thinks of it too fondly,
it may cease to exist
altogether?

Māmā, why do we speak so little
these days?

alone at the back of this Greyhound,
I look over the 401 as little fires
the size of moths   erupt

on an epithelial film of sky
like fireworks, but not quite
– soft columns of light

criss-crossing over distant roads,
farms, dilapidated swingsets,
telephone wires, and lakes

falling, unloading, expanding,
rooting, settling, teaching,

rehabilitating,

bodiless.

HOLOGRAM

in fertile floodlight
fabric lifts to pardon my
cynicism, my pisiform

jutting out in the shape of
a swollen tilapia – another
statistic pushing me past

dilapidated city puddles and
their half-lit blueprints
past the trophic lid of West Dundas

where the Blue Bay Café
lived before it was
permanently closed

where I return in these
terraqueous hours to find
a figure floating

above the telephone wires
arriving and departing in lambent strobes:

> a hologram, weaving between flame trees
> a mother, unlearning how to love

each time I turn
she is gone, and each time
she is gone

she flickers between ridges
in urban wind
laying tiles in the sky

      heels dripping roseate light
      chanting

                ansam, pli pou les départs
                your body is a reservoir
                a repertoire of ashes ossified
                by chloric stains and subaltern
                heat, overlap, overlap with us
                phlebotomize your chronic
                state and rise again with
                us, rise again with water
                we won't wait for you

she bows her head.
she is luminous.

LESSONS IN SOUTHERN TIDES

i.

Pereybere, 1988

does it come back alive, slow wilt
daily routine slung over garden fences?

resist the turn of the hour   seethe
elderberry on gas, let your soft-thrum fingers

pound black roots. water glistens on our necks
like airplane wings blinking helio-confessions

uniting us with our terrified, grounded selves
until dawn comes and we salvage all we can

of this latent rain.

stand here on a terraform cliff
interrogating trees

this must be alive,
cradled by ocean crags, hemolustrous

palms whirl overtongue – ansam, pli.
we are a caged chorus of island fires raging

on the edge of a flat-plated sea.

we spent last June peeling
water droplets and overripe fruit   taste

terminal velocity   taste
our sister islands break loose from seabed

barely alive,
they flicker between raindrops –

those lime-lit lime-coral, lime-eyed
women asleep in the room upstairs.

in a biotic bedtime story
does it come back alive,

virga simmering in the middle
of our lives?

they say the rain is wider
where the women are wearier

so we assume it must be alive, *all of it*
in its perpetual fluidity.

ii.

Lascelles, 2013

come back alive,

night moth crashing
through southern Québec.

in its wake, maps wail open
in weedlight   loosen

wind belts   undulate
on coastal fissures   curl

into warm tile   exhale
through bare soles   lie

here in the shadow
of this garden fence   swell

swell, recede

we have seen this before
hurtling into mind's eye:

a rain-washed rhythm
frayed by oil and sun

rolling with hightide:
this long, charred life

furled into a solitary seawave
tapering on light

how swiftly it cools

how lonesome its roil

how effortless its return.

EULOGY FOR ROADKILL ON A YUKON SOLSTICE

a wound pulsates under
noonday sun, draining blood

and silt over expired dogwood.
a spruce tree moans – hollow, static

highway signs bow toward Dawson City
in angles just short of true.

two miles from the road,
I run my fingers over Selia's back

in search of a protocol for memory,
to collect the cinder flowing

from every chalice in the room,
condense it all to a single moment.

the deer wails.
entropy unspools.

downstairs, Selia delivers a eulogy
as I soak sinew in lime dye,

trace probabilities in circles
over a waxing moon.

its rind glistens with cartels, women,
species whose tendons   diffract

in the arctic flume.
an oceanic devolution.

I fall asleep to the sound of rain.
Selia lights a candle and privately,

we ache for the day we no longer hold
our mothers accountable for who we are.

time in its tectonic sky waives tradition,
heaves with the waning of the moon.

of desire, sexuality: each pigment
strikes the sky, a tonal clamour

before it trickles down quasi-shelves,
rests between us.

the animal keels at our doorway, brume in its antlers,
its bones viscous, dipped in cold clockwork.

Selia knows how to sculpt the water
that leaks from dying bodies.

with tenderness, she collects droplets from a thaw
three continents away, two hand spans away,

one bedpost away, repeating –
there is no distance that aches more than a year.

now she is cold, and the deer has regressed
to oily rain and carbon earth.

the water is narcotic. it pools
on the underside of the evening.

and when I open my eyes, I see
their bodies reflected upside down

in raindrops on my windowpane,
dissolving in the northern hemisphere.

THAW

snow
  drips from suburban eaves,
    each fractal a bead of raw muscle
      embracing last year's moss in a departed

motion.
  our bloodline is sequential to
    city thaws. it glances over tax returns
      and ticket stubs, nestles in the margins of old

anther
  beyond concrete bibles, tile ridges
    and rigid stairwells. cities have a way of
      exposing my indelicacy, my atrophic mind

trailing
  between the mouths of sacrifice and
    deep recall, jaundiced winter and spring
      thaws. in my coffee cup, helices clot together in

genetic
  archipelagos, theories I will revisit
    after spring's apologetic return, once
      the sea splits into biographies. outside, tar

liquefies
  in distended light and finally
    the crocus buds break loose.
      children laugh between lanes of traffic in

traffic
  and I resume my ceremony
    trip over ribbons of southern moons
      search the eyes of strangers on subway cars:

do you remember what it sounds like
to be alone and hear a sunbird
darting through sugarcane?

YEAR OF THE LAMB

that night, the trees folded in hypnotic hulls

splinters on a wind pocked by lantern glow

the year unravelled in solemn hush

swift as nails driven into wet wood

what began as a premonition – a sheen on our wrists

an overripe orange

broke in my chest, a catalysis rebirthed

the laundry in our yard scorched

orchids delayed their total flash

a mathematical rejection for ants

filing along the back wall toward

a funeral we could not see taking place

~

motel room on the outskirts of Montréal

my twenty-eighth lunar new year

Pépin, we were nothing but lambs dipped in gunpowder

I wring tidal flats from static air

we didn't know it then but that was our life

I lay firecrackers over sheets

I kneel to collect the debris of decades

shaken loose from foreign floorboards.

~

where are you hiding

in the cordgrass and sugarcane

in the corrugated slums of a heat-slashed city

in the cortical mass of bluebird wreckage

in the choral lilt of schoolgirls on dirt streets

in the corporeal chants of underwater stairways

in the cordialities littering Wàipó's funeral

in the coral limbs beneath the bedframe

in the choroid flare of insects

in the courts that vaulted us toward a life of perpetual trembling

~

don't tell me the breaking is the release

for you are half the reason I fear the ocean

the ocean which arcs into sundrift like

a child learning triangles in a dark summer

tinfoil legs keeling between water and sky

in blood and bone we are rags on earth

slivers of semi-consciousness dotting the space

between two unknowns

~

when midnight comes, snow falls to the carpet

in a chronological ribbon: a bibliography of women

bobbing in succession to the surface

of the Indian Ocean, eyes wide, grinning

unblinking under callused sun

like those spider lilies that used to sprout

at the foot of my bed: trapeze artists lancing clouds

with crooked wrists.

FUNERAL

hyaline surface
of Lake Ontario
swirls in the wake
of a passing ferry

place of coming
of going, of the
regurgitation
of entire peoples

is this our shared
birthplace, wilting
outside of us?
cold continent,

resume
your traditional
exorcism on the logic
of leaving

corroded
by coastal rain:
an old abacus
this critical mass

the paintings
I found beneath
the bed.

the urn between
my palms pulses
on southern water
cycles

behind me, Māmā
spills her wine.

when I tilt Wàipó's ashes
to the lake, they touch
earth at the centre
of each of its

abandoned tremors.

PART III

PRECIPITATE

But I will escape for now, inert on the warm cement... carry me up, take me to the pinnacle of the great mountain chains... beyond Chamarel with its earth sick colours, and where life begins.

– Marie-Thérèse Humbert

THE LIGHTHOUSE KEEPER OF POINTE AUX SABLES

i.

south of sutured harbours
in the hydric rill of swallows
and swollen bulbs of rain, where
bodies usher bodies into being,
Wàipó presses floors to sleep
the anchors in her blood
tightened by riparian blooms

she says to herself,
did you notice the oil and grain
on the loading dock, sugar estate
phantoms burnt on moth silk
the burly men on rum rows,
dancing

> in what billowed cure will birth amass,
> aquatic prayers rise to another red eclipse?

along a perennial strip of sand
she marks in code her cyclic act
before boats, tiny and ripped,
arrive in chiselled throes
offering slabs of planetary tile,
all marble, topaz, and rose-gold
merely surviving, emboldened
by modern tides and orange groves
marred by the winged will to possess.

ii.

what survives the ethanolic boom
of island breath?
there were churches pulped in light
and dancers in the marshland,
pruning the oculi of southern clouds
from which entire neighbourhoods dripped
in orbs:
concrete and mango juice, laundry
and barefoot schoolgirls, all
pooling at the centre of a tilted field

she says to herself,
brace for impact. there is no hierarchy
to the rooms of tall trees
wrists bound to wrists,
the boats lie blistered on anchors
parallel to those she ran aground
time and again,
agent of the vague mountain
where the last living cypress curdles into old
village networks, oventops alive and lighted by
the creaking flyby of cosmic crows.

iii.

in this high cedarwood room,
what can she say of such non-arrival?
of the cold bio-simmer of salt?

she says to herself,
what a sight from way up here.
beam the searchlight: cranial fluid
erupts on the offing
seeping south southern still –
my mother's mother,
author of disaster
crouching in a blackened window.

OIL SPILL II

metallic water rolls inland   *deluge of slick*
reflected on filtered clouds   *pristine shorelines*
solar effigy, nearly cosmic   *hundreds of tonnes*
the half-lives of ecosystems   *ecological disaster*
etched to the hulls of cargo   *mangrove skeletons*
ships, polyps burst, my TV   *people donate hair*
flashes over sterile skylines   *declares emergency*
I sit still as newscast photos   *islanders donate hair*
seep through my living room   *spill worsens*
algae erodes the carpet, lifts   *update – captain charged*
palms to soil, shoal to root   *crude oil*
the plume thickens, creeps   *thousands of species*
knocks   *government sinks boat*

mama showed up at my door   *dolphins wash up*
for the first time in months   *protests in Port Louis*
face sunk in orange light   *together*
scalp smooth and round   *pray*
hair folded in a plastic bag   *ansam*
hey, help me mail this   *pli*

at the corners of the continental shelf
seagrass suffocates in synthetic riffs
do not tell me, it says
that the architecture of
this ocean is not built
upon the backs of weary islanders.

on the other side of the world
a mailing stamp
sets a body
back in motion.

RECURRING SEAM

and it returned, and it ruptured
the semiotic lightness of sleep
an estuary curdling under the mantle

of my conscience, my restless mind
threaded by chloral wind, I am quite
certain this time – basaltic rockface

torn by an angry sea, fleets of zebra doves
banking above on blackened wind
the flash of coral just below the waves

burnt and grafted, the pull of sunbeams
bruised and bold, the island, its topology
its leaning strata, its volcanic centre

stretch marks on a thigh coursing
between cracks on a delicate strip of time,
on silicate sheets, something else

is stirring beneath the waves:
a hand, reaching
hair, grasping

creaking
dripping

down the hall, creole whispers hush,
slip beneath a leaf.

SIX THUNDERSTORMS IN CHINATOWN

i.
what do I recall of faces retracted
to storage rooms? skin homed to
cloth, milk crates pocked by tar,
redundant only in mind's eye with
those metallic birds they said
would be gone by winter.

ii.
on a besoin d'cette pluie! men yell
over iron grates, tossing fruit peels
downwind. *we need this rain!*
the wind curls. our arms recoil
to crèche-black linen.

iii.
roads striated with runlets and glass
orbit us in desperate licks. let this
water reveal our houses,
the bent bodies within.

iv.
Māmā crouches beneath the eaves with
other alleyway hires. unborn children
prowl the street. this is our quiet
devolution, raw and lustrous
in its countless moral
configurations.

v.
the hour is a bowl of bodies
rocking with heartsick alms.
we bow our heads as thunder
resumes its ceremony, cracking
our skins to unrecognizable husks.

vi.
when the rain stops, she collects
her clothes. All too soon
and all too causal, birds
rise in great radial flocks:
pricks of blood on the surface
of a startled island.

CIRCADIAN RAIN

slip through citrine gravel. in after-rain,
alleyways dilate. a single trash heap
twitches and stills like a damaged cloud.

in after-rain, the city devolves. no longer
alive in its natural mechanics, but cleansed
to a single lustrous layer: a damp sheet

exposing all things dead and dying. part this
curtain of after-rain, olivine air. in the alley
behind my apartment, a liminal mass:

a chrysalis plastered to brick, soaked in laundry
fumes. a fugitive whittled by after-rain
dislocated from wind-streams, from

a corridor in the sky

when I pull her free, love, or recognition
catches in my throat
and stings.

there is no pulse in an open palm
no footsteps upstairs. there is only this, us –
our failed rescue from the diplomacy

of clouds. inside her lifeless cocoon,
the austral currents   converge

and I resist the urge to   crush.

RECIPE FOR A SOUTHERN CYCLONE

Note: To yield a perfect cyclone, it must be August. This recipe is best followed in the evening. In the evening, grief changes colour.

INGREDIENTS
one jar
freshly peeled ginger root
freshly grated horseradish
one chopped onion
a handful of garlic cloves
zest from a lemon
turmeric and cayenne powder
½ litre of apple cider vinegar
raw honey
A quiet place to mourn

INSTRUCTIONS
1. Fill the glass with apple cider vinegar and place it on the table. Forget the rest.
2. Dip your finger inside; it is important that this be done with as much restraint as possible.
3. Twirl your finger, slowly, then quickly, then mournfully – though most forgo the latter. Bend, flex until your skin feels like fire pulled taut over a rockface.
4. Amber cyclones will form. Don't be alarmed. They will reflect on the ceiling, touch down somewhere in the Indian Ocean.
5. Lift your finger from the glass – think pigeons in the wake of morning, dripping blood.

6. Hear yourself exhale as your finger hits the table, feel yourself begin to sweat because somewhere in the Indian Ocean, a church door is swinging open and boats are beating up against pale sandbeds. Don't be alarmed.

7. Every layer of the sky will bristle. Don't be alarmed.

8. Resist the urge to wipe your hand on a tea towel. Resist the urge to curse. It is not your job to be upset. This is latent.

9. The bark will fall from trees. Don't be alarmed.

10. Stray dogs will turn in circles until their heads become their tails and they shrivel into wheatgrass. Resist the urge to scrub. This is irreparable.

11. Now if you squint across the hemispheres you might see her – a woman sinking into the water somewhere in the Indian Ocean, rigid, foot-first, a sad smile wavering. Until it is just her hair resting on the surface – a thousand water snakes billowing from the top of a bottle.

12. Don't be alarmed. Remember that this is not new.

TRIMESTERS

I am sitting in a cafe in Fredericton
the waitress is pregnant

she says
are you all finished

I cannot see the expression
on her face

will you stay, is what she means
but we are both

thinking about the storm
outside, the botanic tableau

of window foliage
acacia, rosebush, tulips

eviscerated by droplets
their long shadows

perched at the base
of my spine, merely to

show how hollow
it has been

over here, all these years
carbon-dating photos

in back rooms where
resistance has become

my valence
weightless, fallen homes

clatter through my head
to fortify, to lift my

eyelids back to sun
so ciliate, so slow

where meadows exist
as vacuums for

dispossession, city names
as lesions for design

this language a pathology
a plight from control

straining in the space between
Ignore All and Add to Dictionary

parallel to our own
dose-response curve.

'Nautical Disaster'
plays on the stereo

our reflections
in the wet glass

I respond
sorry, yes. yes thank you

the waitress bends down
starts, and chuckles

one hand on her belly
the other in mindless service

oh, she's a kicker!

the rain thickens,
sharpens its teeth.

standing at the edge of the rockface, I look down to the swimming hole at Trou aux Cerfs. bodies move in filtered whirls, laughing, glistening. In this dream I am alive and on the island for the first time in five decades. I am alive and standing at

the edge of the rockface asks me how I experienced entire lives: as road silt, as periodic wildfires, as phone calls to Māmā and the growing space between them. stray dogs wander in and out of view, outlaws panting under clouds. I want to wrest my skin from ice, return it to its birthplace, to translucence, on the mild side of guava season I am standing at the edge of

the rockface guides me and as I leap, the faces below yell *no, no, bad spot, pala!* but I am in the water and my feet scrape shoal, sharp and shallow. for the brief moment I am submerged, I hear a motorboat underwater, high-pitched and far away. when I surface, my feet come up as honeycombs flecked with blood, with dark coral, and rock, and clay, and the way

I experienced entire lives: as absence.

CICADAS

pooling in a salt marsh, thirty years
away from my father's second wife,

I study the lifecycle of cicadas.
inside, the super-8 reels on a sunken tv

pills spin in their orange containers,
and photographs on the fridge turn white.

I watch as water rolls into itself,
into decades, into a statue of Krishna

exhaling from his feet. glasswork spills
through the seasons, a skylight

pushing. a pillowcase, wilting
on a deerfly dipped in dirty water

carrying wafts of ginseng into
tomorrow's wake.

as if on cue, cicadas come loose
from the dark side of the evening

their exoskeletons erupting
to tephral sand, like
                    a jar of fire cider vinegar, cracked open too soon

staining her dress
celestial.

WHEN SHE STOPPED ME AT THE GAS
STATION IN HAUTES-PLAINES

I had just swallowed my meds.
it was minus twenty-seven.

she asked me
        how is the new house? how is your mother?

seasons ago, she mouthed it from
across a dinner table lined with strangers –
        have you already forgotten the taste of dholl puri?

her face contorted under sterile lamps
when she moved, her hair rained hail

and washer fluid, percolated with gasoline
hips corroded on a tensile bed of salt

a ravanne droned on the west end
volcanic material stirred

in the foundations of snow-bludgeoned
homes, suburban brick

I had to leave

she knew me too well –
        did you forget about guava season?

ice cracked with artificial history –
    you know Le Morne is shrinking back into the ocean.
    even a mountain knows it is okay to begin again.

I swiped my card. headlights glared.
we were a ballad, quaking inside the last gas

light in the city. my car door slammed.

she turned –
    don't forget how to stay.
    no matter how many times you need to leave,
    don't forget how to stay.

as I pulled away, I tried to keep her in sight
to track where she had come from
to track where she was going next

but all I could see was

    my reflection in the rear-view

evaporating.

ROOM SERVICE

in the eye of a billboard off the cracked highway
mango trees lean northward
      a faithful tribute to all things
      too frail to exist
the woman in Apartment Three shaves her head
into a Ziploc bag, sheet metal fingers twitching
      her sweat plummets through water cycles throbs
      in the gallows of trees   pools
at the gnawed doors to her grandchildren's lives
would this life have remitted, had we embraced
the rules of reciprocity
      the prowling hiss of weathervanes
      engorged, leaning lichen-wet fuselage
wiped from the corners of our mouths
this tender decomposition, this   lull
      on a nodal flame, the brittle will to love

outside, the clouds splinter   translate
gently to television static
      the satellite dish on the roof
      murmurs in languages of salt
quiescent
until the figurine elk

      sinking perpetually in the Indian Ocean

touches sand.

PART IV

COLLECT

that dynamic indeterminacy that flourishes, like porcelain coral, where senses meet the undersea.

– Killian Quigley

MĀMĀ, WHERE DOES YOUR LIGHT LEAK?

before we dissolve
I bow before the women who drain quietly
from decades before us

ask their bodies to remember
the taste of steel, the rush
of cloud traffic

I never told you, Māmā
but the summer before Wàipó died
I swam every morning
beneath the Champlain Bridge

the dock dipped: a year
in osmotic return
tethered to the underside
of a ramshackle moon

my mouth parted
on a vacant shoulder.

the colour of water
at four in the morning has no name
its ripples coated in dialects
of recourse

perhaps it is

Forgotten
or Lapsed
or Je Suis Encore Là.

when it carried me under
it drew behind my left eye
a fable from long ago –

     the feeling of being nothing, yet vibrating
      in the key of a drowsy metropole.

     ~

I met a woman once whose head was smoother than the wine spilled at her funeral. she came in a bundle of plastic tubes, thought she could hear a baby in the clock on the hospital wall. the creases in her pillow tapered into white caps stilled mid-grin, aching to curl over dead seasons, hollowed vessels, an abandoned lighthouse.

she was at once the room itself and all the emptiness it held.

I took her bruises in my palm as she plotted the coordinates
    of memory:

dead lime tree
                                broken bottles of motel shampoo

                    dying turtle
et cetera   paintbrushes
                            lost wedding vow

        seatbelt signals   fire cider   cigarette butts

                    paper moths taped to the rear-view

            injured dog
                                soggy dictionary

            a fine horsehair comb   milkweed tulle

            brass urn
                                        spoiled papaya
                        damp floorboards
immigration stamp   fossilized paint

                    lukewarm Fanta
        plane water   et cetera
                            jar of hair

            et cetera   amber-stained fingertip
                    lunar calendar

                            ～

her monitors traced blueprints
of Beau-Bassin, angled
with a precision known
only to dust particles

dust soaked in siren light

dust switching the channel to ballet

dust rearranging the room as I slept by her bed

dust reminding me, Māmā –

although it is your mother dying, I know it is all of us at once.

~

Māmā,
remember when you thought I was allergic
to light?

remember how you would close
the bathroom door   rock
me slow until the crack of gold
beneath your feet
disappeared?

you drew atlases on my back:
say Trou aux Cerfs, say Pereybere
until your lessons encircled the earth
streamlets flowing down the continent
like frightened plovers

your voice returns, morse code
in my walls, spins circles
in the windowpane

I have donned bodies
unlearned the signatures
of rainclouds

yet no matter how often I fold
my limbs into Québec rivers,

I cannot peel from my skin
the layer that is you.

~

crack open my middle name.
Valérie.

the almost name
the gold-dipped sari, ocean-strapped
pregnant-at-seventeen name.

the murmurings of a dying woman
wedged between my letters

        is it any wonder we bathe in foreign skins
           when no one is watching?

histories no more familiar than the letters they fill
spinning the hourglasses
in rhododendron roots
at the crest
    of every hour.

it's coming up silver
chalice wax coats the pews.

the women in the sky
in the mired city, in the frozen fields
are bowing their heads
in an elegy to you,
Māmā.

I hear them sometimes
when the night is quiet
chanting in unison –

how to say
wait for me
in creole?

~

the nurse opens the curtain to give her light. she lifts her neck, slowly. softly. with restraint. just outside her window, milkweed splits into October, spinning tulle into gold sky. when she speaks, her words leap forth into dim, and I am beset with an old memory, though I cannot tell if it is really mine: shadows of birds darting into sugarcane.

the ballerinas on screen sprout wings and flutter into the ceiling fan, where they burst into two thousand feathers each. why do we ascribe such unbound wisdom to dying bodies?

I reach under her pillow in search of where your light leaks and my hand falls through empty space.

~

Māmā,
what did the woman in the hospital do to you?

I have been sitting in this bus shelter for hours
reading about the dynamics of flight

waiting for the sun to recall its ancestry
to drip down stairways on a softer horizon

in graceful defeat learned from the renewal of water.

> *tann ma*
> *wait for me*

this is a careful extraction.

this
is a loveless
dance.

ACKNOWLEDGEMENTS

Previous iterations of these poems have appeared in *The Malahat Review*, *Grain*, PRISM International, *Arc Poetry Magazine*, *Gutter*, *Middleground*, *Plenitude Magazine*, and *Canadian Notes & Queries*. A special thank you to the editors of these publications.

The following works were helpful in the writing of this book: *The Aesthetics of the Undersea*, edited by Margaret Cohen and Killian Quigley, *Tiger in Paradise: Reading global Mauritius in shifting space and time* by N. L. Aumeerally, and *Postcolonial ecocriticism, island tourism and the geopoetics of beach* by Namrata Poddar.

The writing of this work was supported in part by the Writer's Trust of Canada Mentorship Program. Thank you to Liz Howard for her reassurance, her keen attention to detail, and for asking the right questions. Thanks to James Davies from the Trust.

A deep thanks to Susan Holbrook for her guidance and patience. Thank you to Alana Wilcox, James Lindsay, Crystal Sikma, and the incredible Coach House Team for carrying this book with such immense kindness and belief.

Thank you to Carolyn Smart for her unwavering support. To Stuart Ross and John Elizabeth Stintzi for their cheer and words of encouragement. To my friends for reading this work at its various stages: Kinzy, Ellen, Anthony, Maysam, Seb, Donavan, Julia, Hannah, and Aidan. Thanks to my family: to Popo and Kung Kung, to Adrian Kiva. To my wonderful parents Alan and Jill, and to Skylar, Natara, and Dominic.

RHIANNON NG CHENG HIN was born in Edinburgh, Scotland, and lives in Ottawa. Her poetry has been published in *Gutter*, *The Malahat Review*, *Grain*, *Arc Poetry Magazine*, and elsewhere, and she currently serves as Associate Poetry Editor with *Plenitude Magazine*. She holds a Master's degree in Environmental Toxicology from the University of Ottawa. *Fire Cider Rain* is her debut collection.

Typeset in Arno and Artifex Hand.

Printed at the Coach House on bpNichol Lane in Toronto, Ontario, on Zephyr Antique Laid paper, which was manufactured, acid-free, in Saint-Jérôme, Quebec, from second-growth forests. This book was printed with vegetable-based ink on a 1973 Heidelberg KORD offset litho press. Its pages were folded on a Baumfolder, gathered by hand, bound on a Sulby Auto-Minabinda, and trimmed on a Polar single-knife cutter.

Coach House is on the traditional territory of many nations including the Mississaugas of the Credit, the Anishnabeg, the Chippewa, the Haudenosaunee, and the Wendat peoples, and is now home to many diverse First Nations, Inuit, and Métis peoples. We acknowledge that Toronto is covered by Treaty 13 with the Mississaugas of the Credit. We are grateful to live and work on this land.

Edited for the press by Susan Holbrook
Cover and interior design by Crystal Sikma
Author photo by Jasmine Acharya

Coach House Books
80 bpNichol Lane
Toronto ON M5S 3J4
Canada

416 979 2217
800 367 6360

mail@chbooks.com
www.chbooks.com